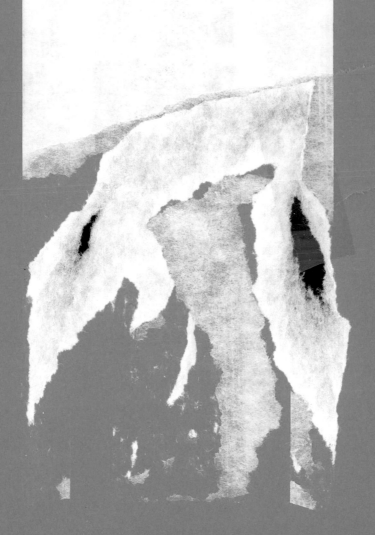

Impressionist Picnics

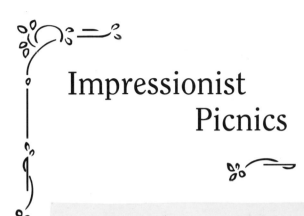

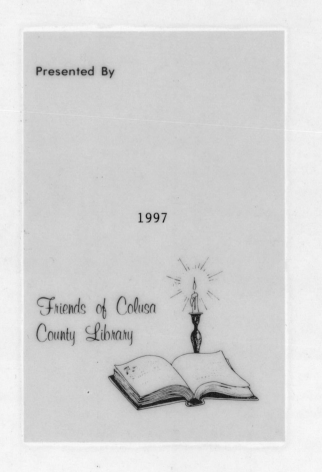

Presented By

1997

Friends of Colusa
County Library

Édouard Manet, Le Déjeuner sur l'Herbe, *1863. Musée d'Orsay, Paris.*

Painters & Food

Impressionist
Picnics

by
Gillian Riley

Pomegranate Artbooks
San Francisco

First published 1993 by Pomegranate Artbooks
Box 6099, Rohnert Park, California 94927

Conceived, designed, and produced by
New England Editions Limited
25 Oakford Road
London, NW5 1AJ, England

Library of Congress Catalog Card Number 93-84102

ISBN: 1–56640–580–7

10 8 6 4 2 1 3 5 7 9

Editor/Art Director: **Treld Pelkey Bicknell**

Book Design: **Gillian Riley**

Jacket/cover Design: **Glynn Pickerill**

Typeset in Clearface by **The R & B Partnership**

Printed in Singapore by **Imago Publishing**

Contents

Introduction
Scents & Shimmering Visions...

The idea of a picnic, a spontaneous, improvised meal out of doors with friends, appeals to us in the same way as the paintings of the Impressionists. We—neither artists, nor critics, nor chefs—enjoy the fresh colors and the atmosphere, cheerfully unaware of the underlying structures. However, "There are certain days," wrote Emile Zola, "when beyond the scents and the shimmering visions...I glimpse the hard outlines of things as they are."

Until quite recently the structure of a serious French picnic was more like that of a conventional meal. The hard outlines mattered. The carefree young Parisians spread decoratively on the grass in Monet's *Déjeuner sur l'Herbe* are about to settle down to a complete lunch provided by one of the astute *traiteurs*, who laid on everything the holidaymakers could possibly want when they got off the train at one of the stations on the new line from the Gare St. Lazare. The complete range of china, glass, cutlery, table linen, as well as appropriate food and wine, was borne to the appointed spot by helpful servants, one of whom is seen crouching deferentially behind a tree on the right.

And so it was with the paintings. We enjoy them today for their "impressions" of the pleasures of everyday life, of fleeting atmospheric moments captured in rapid blobs and streaks of paint and, it must be confessed, for their period charm—the striped silk dresses in the Luxembourg Gardens, and the crowded cafés and bars on the boulevards of Haussmann's brave new Paris. The disciplines of formal composition and the skillful professionalism of the painting are there, taken for granted, like the solid traditions of French cuisine which are responsible for all those good things we snatch from *charcuterie* and market stall as we dash for a picnic in the fresh air.

This ideal of the picnic is celebrated in so many paintings outside the strict definition of Impressionism that I felt able to include works by the most unlikely people in this anthology. From Toulouse-Lautrec to de Segonzac, with contributions in the right spirit from Vuillard and Bonnard and recipes from writers as far apart as "Tante Marie" and Alice B. Toklas.

The group of painters we now know as *Impressionists* included Claude Monet, Auguste Renoir, Camille Pissarro, Alfred Sisley, Frédéric Bazille, Berthe Morisot, and the friends and colleagues most closely associated with them such as Édouard Manet, Edgar Degas, and Mary Cassatt. They had links with painters as far apart as Whistler and Cézanne, Bonnard, Vuillard and Orpen.

To pin down such an amorphous group of people with a neat label to cover their artistic style and food preferences is clearly absurd. So different in so many ways, perhaps what they all had most in common was their love of the outdoors, with its clarity, light, freedom, and immediacy of sensation.

Toulouse-Lautrec, for example, would never have considered himself an Impressionist. He was bored with landscape. "The figure is everything, landscape should never be more than an accessory..." But his zest for life, in particular the pleasures of eating and drinking, drew him into a close web of friendships and social gatherings which included patrons, dealers, writers, and musicians. Thadée and Misia Natanson entertained Bonnard, Vuillard, and Toulouse-Lautrec for long weekends at their country homes, where relaxed breakfasts and informal lunches on the terrace were often recorded in photographs and sketches by their faithful house guests.

Manet's notorious *Déjeuner sur l'Herbe* is the picnic picture that spurred them on. What shocked critics and public to the core was not so much the naked woman and her equivocal relationship with the smart young men lounging by her carelessly discarded clothes, but the outdoor setting and the flamboyantly casual execution of the painting. The food was peripheral. Much later Henri le Sidaner painted a mysterious picnic without people, Cézanne attempted an exercise on a classical theme, Pissarro's daughter sketched Madame Cézanne preparing a fry-up for a mixed bunch of Impressionists, and Morisot painted her daughter and husband having an elegant little meal on the grass.

The gastronomy changed, but the spirit of the picnic, a light-hearted attitude to eating and drinking, remains an inspiration to us when thoughts of cooking nudge us towards pretentiousness or pomposity.

The pleasures of eating out in France are only surpassed by the delights of preparing meals at home. The profusion of good things in markets, butchers, bakers, and *charcuteries* is a temptation to every cheerful hedonist or compulsive cook. The picnic meal, indoors or outdoors, is a way of taking possession of this glowing cornucopia of fruit, cheeses, bread, pâtés, quiches, patisserie, and wine. But the freedom of a friendly kitchen allows greater scope; a fat free-range chicken, a handful of sorrel, a heap of yellow *girolles*, and good advice from market woman or shopkeeper and the inquisitive cook, innovative or traditional, can learn in a relaxed, holiday spirit—with neither trials nor errors—something about the rich gastronomic traditions celebrated so evocatively by the artists in this book.

The recipes that accompany the paintings are an idiosyncratic selection of dishes I have enjoyed preparing in various hospitable kitchens in France—from wet Sundays in Bergerac to a July heatwave in a deserted Montparnasse. The traditions of classic French cooking have been explained with greater lucidity by the authors mentioned in the Bibliography, but I hope that my own enthusiasm will encourage others to enjoy recreating some of the sensations inspired by the Impressionist approach to food and eating.

GILLIAN RILEY, 1993

Claude Monet, Le Déjeuner sur l'Herbe, (detail) *1865-66. Musée d'Orsay, Paris.*

Young Monet's Respectable Outing

Pâté en Croûte
Chicken With Tarragon

Camille Doncieux, Claude Monet's (1840-1926) mistress, loved engraved fashion plates, and Monet enjoyed painting her in the striped and spotted muslin and silk dresses advertised in them. She and his friend Frédéric Bazille posed for most of the characters in his *Déjeuner sur l'Herbe*, but the really important subjects of this painting are the shimmering sunlight and dappled shadows on the silver birches in the forest of Fontainebleau.

Inspired by Manet's version of the same subject, the younger artist embarked, in the summer of 1865, on the ambitious theme of life-sized, ordinary people enjoying themselves in the open air. Such a banal, everyday event—with no academic or mythological content, and set out of doors—was anathema to critics and the art establishment. The project was deemed a failure. Monet decamped, leaving in his wake the usual cloud of debts and unpaid bills. The unfinished painting deteriorated, rolled up in a corner of Bazille's studio.

Years later Monet salvaged the central portion of the painting and hung it in his studio in Giverny. It was a reminder of those carefree days before the movement—of which he was to become the most illustrious member—had even acquired a name, and the ambitious young painters who met at the Café Guerbois were still hoping to get their paintings hung in the respectable Salon.

The young middle-class people who swarmed out of Paris into the previously peaceful countryside were by no means all painters and bohemians. The bathing place and restaurant La Grenouillère was in a calm backwater of the Seine near Bougival. There, trainloads of day-trippers could embark on the short boat trip to the picturesque landing stage and totter along the precarious walkway to the tiny island, affectionately known as the Camembert. An ephemeral moment was caught by Monet and Renoir before the restaurant was destroyed in a fire in 1869.

The food enjoyed on these expeditions would have been the conventional fare of middle class homes and restaurants. Monet's picnic includes a pâté en croûte, a cold chicken, fruit, wine, and quantities of plates and cutlery—nothing like the imaginative sandwiches devised by Alice B. Toklas for her intrepid outings in Gertrude Stein's two-seater open Ford roadster, seventy years later (see page 87).

Claude Monet, Bathing at La Grenouillère, *1869. The National Gallery, London.*

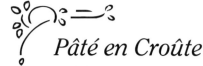

Pâté en Croûte

This does not have to be cooked in a pastry crust, but is easier to handle on a picnic if you do.

For the crust:

1 lb. (500 g) plain flour

8 oz. (250 g) lard (see pages 90 and 91)

Mix together with 1 teaspoon salt and moisten with enough water to make a stiff paste. Roll out.

For the filling:

1 lb. (500 g) lean shoulder of pork

1/2 lb. (250 g) fat pork belly

1/2 lb. (250 g) *pancetta* or dry-cured, unsmoked bacon (see page 90)

1 medium sized onion, chopped

2 oz. (60 g) butter

1 tablespoon flour (see page 91)

1 glass dry wine, red or white

2 teaspoons freshly ground spices, including some or all of the following, depending on your preferences: cinnamon, nutmeg, cloves, black peppercorns, and juniper berries

1/2 teaspoon thyme

4 cloves of garlic, peeled and chopped

Salt to taste

Cut the meat and bacon very fine with a sharp knife. This takes time but is better than using a mincer. Marinate overnight in the wine, salt, and 1 teaspoon of the spices.

Next day, sauté the onions in the butter until soft, stir in the flour and cook for a few minutes. Moisten with a little more wine to make a thick mixture. Stir this into the marinated meat, adding the reserved spices.

Line a terrine or baking tin with the pastry, keeping some by for a lid. Tip in the pâté mixture. Cover with a pastry lid, moistening the edges to seal carefully. Decorate the top with something creative—leaves or a lattice pattern. Make a hole for the steam to get out.

Bake in a moderate oven for about 1½ hours, cover the pastry with foil if it looks like browning. Cool for half an hour before removing from the tin or terrine.

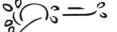

Chicken with Tarragon

1 free range chicken, 2½ - 3 lbs (1.25 - 1.5 kg)
1 bunch tarragon
Garlic to taste, whole cloves peeled
1 glass dry white wine and additional water
Salt and pepper

Stuff half the tarragon inside the chicken, push some of the rest between the legs and breast. Add as much garlic as you like. Salt and pepper well. Put the wine in the bottom of an ovenproof pot and add the chicken. Cook, covered, in a medium oven for 1 to 1½ hours, or on top of the stove, adding more wine or water if necessary. Do not overcook.

When done, (the legs should waggle loosely when prodded), leave to cool in the cooking juices.

For a formal picnic, complete with lavish accoutrements, carve on the spot, with a flourish. Otherwise cut up the bird beforehand and make up into portions on disposable plastic plates, cling-wrapped, which can be handed round to the hungry. If this seems too depressingly like airline food, stay at home and eat it in comfort with your feet under the table.

Édouard Vuillard, Lunch at Villeneuve-sur-Yonne, *c. 1902 and 1934. Meals out of doors are a constant theme in Impressionist and Post-Impressionist paintings. This work records, in fact, lunch on the terrace of a country house in Vasouy in Normandy, Vuillard reworked it many years later—a nostalgic experience—adding and subtracting old and new friends, with a debonair young Bonnard on the left. The National Gallery, London.*

Pierre-Auguste Renoir, The Luncheon of the Boating Party, *1880-81.*
The Phillips Collection, Washington.

Auguste Renoir's Day on the River

Coq au Vin
Courgette Soufflé

"They took Paris with them wherever they went." This waterside inn, the Restaurant Fournaise at Chatou, catered for chic young Parisians enjoying summer weekends on the river, escaping the noise and bustle of Paris, and creating a cheerful holiday bustle of their own. Auguste Renoir (1841-1919) caught the atmosphere of a late summer in the 1880s in his two paintings of amateur canoeists relaxing over lunch. He contrasted the serious biceps of a real waterman, Alphonse Fournaise—the son of the proprietor, leaning against the balcony on the left—with his eager young clients, all weekend boatmen. Aline Charigot, whom Renoir later married, wore a pretty bonnet based on the straw hats of the oarsmen.

The food was that of the new, fashionable Parisian restaurants, very different from the traditional cooking of country inns like the Auberge of Mère Antoine at Marlotte near Fontainebleau where, back in the 1860s, Renoir had painted a group of young artists in a rustic, unsophisticated setting. A familiar lament was already becoming heard in the land for those unspoilt little places now ruined by trippers, where simple food and a glass of the patron's wine were being replaced by sophisticated menus and décors.

Auguste Renoir, however, seemed quite happy to adapt to Parisian chic in his celebration of everyday life. He painted for pleasure. He didn't expect his luscious models to have brains, and he did not greatly care to sit up all night theorizing about points of style and ending up too hung over for an early start next morning. Back in town after a trip to the country, he would set to work recording the gaiety of life on the boulevards with his clear, bright colors and skillful technique.

17

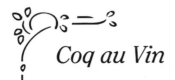

Coq au Vin

1 large free-range chicken cut into joints
1 lb. (500 g) pickling onions
½ lb. (250 g) mushrooms
½ oz. (15 g) dried mushrooms
½ lb. (250 g) *pancetta* or dry-cured, unsmoked, fatty bacon,
    diced (see page 90)
Garlic to taste, 1 whole clove, smashed, for the stock and 4 or
    5, peeled and chopped, for the chicken
Bay leaves, thyme, salt and pepper to taste
Potato or rice flour (optional) (see page 91)
Butter

A good *Coq au Vin* is greater than the sum of its parts. First-class ingredients and an understanding of the process are what you need. The aim is to reduce a bottle of good red wine to a thick, dark, delicious sauce, without boiling to rags the chicken cooked in it. My solution is to joint the chicken and make a stock out of the carcass, a cup of water, half the bottle of wine, and seasonings. Simmer this with the lid off for some of the time, so that you end up with about 2 cups of well-flavored liquid.

Put the chicken joints in a heavy, wide, pan and add the rest of the wine, the stock, bay leaves, thyme, pepper, garlic, and the bacon. Cook, covered, for 30 minutes. Then remove the lid and simmer gently for another 30 minutes.

Meanwhile cook the fresh mushrooms, cut into walnut-sized pieces, in a little butter and a chopped clove of garlic until the juices run out. Turn up the heat so that the juices concentrate. Keep on one side.

Peel the onions in a bowl of warm water (to avoid weeping). Cook them in a heavy-bottomed frying pan with a knob of butter and half a cup of water until the water has evaporated and the onions start to color.

Add the mushrooms and onions to the chicken in the pot and cook together for another 20 minutes, shaking from time to time and watching carefully to make sure the sauce is neither too runny nor too dense. Check at this stage for salt—the bacon will have added a fair amount already.

Mix some potato flour with a little water and add to the pan 10 minutes before serving, stir in gently with plenty of freshly ground black pepper and a knob of unsalted butter.

Serve with plain boiled rice and a green salad. In winter *polenta* (see page 92) goes very well, and any guest feeling the cold can be given the job of stirring the pot of *polenta* for 40 minutes.

Pierre-Auguste Renoir, The Inn of Mother Anthony, *1866. Sisley (in a straw hat) and friends at the end of a rustic lunch at Marlotte, on the edge of the forest of Fontainebleau. National Museum, Stockholm.*

Pierre-Auguste Renoir, The Canoeists' Luncheon, *c.1879. The Art Institute of Chicago*

Courgette Soufflé

Anyone who says that ethereal puff pastry and feather-light soufflés are easy to make omits to mention that they were born with cold hands and a cool head. If, like me, you were born under the Breadmakers' Star you have hot hands, a bad temper, and a capacity amounting to genius for producing soggy pastry, bullet-like dumplings, and solid soufflés. The escape clause for the soufflé is to cover it with Parmesan and a home-made tomato sauce and call it a *sformata* (see page 92).

To feed 4 as a starter
1 lb. (500 g) courgettes (zucchini), grated on the
   cheese grater
4 eggs
2 oz. (60 g) grated Gruyère cheese
1 oz. (30 g) grated Parmesan
1 tablespoon flour (see page 91)
1 oz. (30 g) butter
1 cup milk
Liquid from the courgettes
Salt, pepper, and nutmeg to taste

An hour before making the soufflé, grate the courgettes,
sprinkle with salt and leave to drain in a colander, catching
the juices in a basin. Squeeze to extract as much juice as
possible. Cook for a few minutes without water in a heavy-
bottomed pan until the courgettes are soft.

   Separate the yolks and whites of the eggs, reserving 2 of
the yolks for something else, perhaps the dessert on p. 54.

   Melt the butter and cook the flour in it, add enough of
the courgette juices and milk to make a stiff sauce, and let it
cool for ten minutes.

   In a blender or food processor mix the courgettes, 2 egg
yolks, the sauce, the Gruyère, salt, pepper, and freshly grated
nutmeg.

   Whip the egg whites until good and stiff. Add the
courgette mixture quickly and deftly, slicing downwards into
the bowl, sprinkling the Parmesan in as you go. Tip into a
soufflé dish, or ovenproof container, and stand the dish in a
tin of water to prevent the sides burning. Cook in a hot oven
for 20 to 30 minutes.

Édouard Manet, Café-Concert, *1878. Barmaids, working class girls, and an elderly* flâneur *enjoy a fashionable glass of beer and the entertainment provided by* brasseries *and side-walk cafés. The Walters Art Gallery, Baltimore.*

Édouard Manet
Man About Town

Prunes in Brandy
Prunes with Pork
Salmon with Sorrel Sauce
Rabbit Argenteuil

"Darling, I thought she was you!" said Édouard Manet (1832-83) to his affectionate, very plump wife, Suzanne, who had just caught him ogling a sylph-like maiden in the street. Witty, charming, and elegant, Manet was the archetypal *flâneur* (see page 91), for whom the life of cafe and boulevard might have been invented.

It was a deliberate political act of Emperor Louis Napoleon to make Paris an enjoyable place to be. Pleasure, amusements, and frivolity would distract the hearts and minds of the potential revolutionaries among the crowds of aspiring middle classes pouring into the capital to live and work. The wide boulevards, driven straight through the jumble of narrow streets and alleyways of the old Paris, brought fresh air and light—and convenient avenues for the deployment of troops, ever at the ready to quell signs of political activity or revolt.

Manet, with his sharp intelligence, saw through the corruption of the Second Empire. Some of his paintings were wry, aloof comments on a régime he despised. But, for the most part, his was a detached, sardonic view of a world whose pleasures he enjoyed to the full.

The women of Manet's social class—the wives and daughters of wealthy aristocrats or functionaries—had far less freedom than the dressmakers, florists, barmaids, and shop assistants who spent their leisure in *café concerts*, music halls, and the parks and gardens which were growing by the year. In 1848, Paris had less than fifty acres of gardens and public open spaces but, by 1870, more than 4,500 acres of garden and green spaces had been created within the city.

Édouard Manet, The Plum, *1878. National Gallery of Art, Washington.*

Manet's stunning portraits of the painter Berthe Morisot were painted, fully chaperoned, in his studio. She herself would never have dreamt of a night out at a *bal musette* or the *Moulin de la Galette*. The girls who did, often occupied a somewhat dubious place in society. But the neatly dressed young woman in pink, sitting unaccompanied in a public bar, is not labelled by Manet as good or bad. Her air of pensive resignation is that of someone provided with a sticky plum in brandy and no spoon to eat it with; an unlit cigarette and no matches. His paintings tell no stories and make no judgements—we must make of them what we will.

A *flâneur*, like the writer George Moore, had the best of all possible worlds, spending his days as the cool spectator of the busy social scene centered on the new restaurants and cafés frequented by pleasure-seekers with leisure and money to spend. A new kind of gastronomy evolved to appeal to their cheerful hedonism. Pâtisseries and teashops proliferated.

The elegant cuisine of Escoffier, in the expensive restaurants he pioneered with his colleague, Ritz, was a break with the heavy, ornate banquet tradition of Carême. As the Impressionists grew older and more prosperous, they abandoned the rough country inns and uncouth table manners of their wild youth and settled happily for this smart cuisine in the luxurious resorts and hotels of Normandy and the south of France.

Prunes in brandy

Half fill a wide-mouthed glass jar—the kind that certain brands of fruit juice are sold in works well—with plump prunes. Make a syrup by boiling 6 oz. sugar (180g) and 1/4 pint (150 ml) water for 10 minutes. When it has cooled, pour it into the jar. Top up with brandy or Armagnac and leave for a month or so for the flavor to mature.

Prunes with Pork

1½ lbs. (750 g) pork tenderloin
12 good quality prunes
½ bottle Vouvray
1 cup crème fraîche (see page 91)
Salt, pepper, garlic, and bay leaves to taste
Plain flour
Unsalted butter for frying

The fruitiness, verging on sweetness, of the Vouvray goes well with the musty earthiness of the prunes. Soak them in the wine for an hour or so to plump out, but don't let them get soggy. Simmer for 10 minutes.

Slice the pork tenderloin into ½-inch (12-mm) slices and coat with salt, freshly ground black pepper, and flour. Fry them in a little butter until pale gold. Add to the pan the Vouvray in which the prunes have soaked, the bay leaf, and garlic and bring to the boil. Simmer, uncovered, for about ten minutes, then add the prunes and cook for 5 minutes more. Finally stir in the cream and warm through.

Above Left: Édouard Manet, George Moore in the Café, *1879. The elegant, detached, aloof* flâneur *sits with that newly fashionable, somewhat plebeian beverage, a glass of beer. Metropolitan Museum of Art, New York. Above: Édouard Manet,* Two Girls with Glasses of Beer, *c. 1878. The Burrell Collection, Glasgow. Overleaf: Victor Gilbert,* The Fish Market in the Halles-Centrales, *1881. Pride in the splendors of Paris extended to the flood of fresh provisions which flooded daily into its exuberant markets. Private Collection.*

Édouard Manet, The Salmon, *c. 1868-9. Shelburne Museum, Vermont.*

Salmon with Sorrel Sauce

4 salmon steaks
2 cups sorrel leaves, washed and trimmed
Bitter orange juice (see page 90)
1/2 cup butter
Salt and pepper

Marinate the salmon steaks in bitter orange juice and salt overnight. Cook in a hot oven in an ovenproof dish covered in foil until just done; this should take about 15 to 20 minutes depending on the size of the steaks.

Meanwhile wilt the sorrel leaves in a heavy pan with a knob of the butter. Add any juices from the salmon and stir briskly, adding bits of butter to make a thick sauce. Do not overdo the amount of butter as the salmon is quite rich.

Serve with potatoes cooked in a small amount of water to which, towards the end of cooking, a little garlic and butter have been added. The potatoes should sweat it out for a few minutes to absorb the aromas. (Never boil potatoes and then throw away the water, a waste of flavor *and* vitamins. It can be added to soups and stock.)

Rabbit Argenteuil

2 lbs. (1 kg) wild rabbit joints
2 lbs. (1 kg) asparagus
1 cup heavy cream
A knob of butter
Salt, pepper, and garlic to taste

Cut off the woody base of the asparagus and peel the stems. Tie the asparagus into bunches for ease in handling and cook, with the trimmings, in enough salted water to cover. When done, fish out the bunches and keep on one side. Strain the liquid. In it cook the rabbit joints, with salt and a smashed clove of garlic, until tender. If you want a thick sauce, allow the liquid to reduce during cooking by leaving the pan lid off, or partly so. Cut off the asparagus tips and reserve. Liquidize or sieve the stems and add to the rabbit. Add the cream and butter and stir until the sauce thickens; grate in some black pepper and taste for salt. Serve surrounded by the asparagus tips.

This recipe also works well with chicken.

Édouard Manet, The Bunch of Asparagus, *c. 1880. The market gardens of Argenteuil were famous for their asparagus. Wallraf-Richartz Museum, Cologne.*

Édouard Manet, Berthe Morisot with a Bunch of Violets, *1872.*
Berthe Morisot told her daughter, Julie, many years later, that it
was while painting this portrait that Manet suggested that she
should marry his brother, Eugène, which she did, somewhat to
everyone's surprise, in 1874. He provided exactly the affectionate
support she needed to combine her painting career with that of a
successful wife, mother and society hostess. Petit Palais, Paris.

Berthe Morisot
From Violets to Mexican Rice

Mexican Rice
Tuiles
Moules Bordelaises
Potage Bonne Femme

When George Moore claimed that Impressionism was invented in the cafés and bars of Paris he might have mentioned that the finest painter of the movement never set foot in one. Berthe Morisot (1841-95) came from a comfortably off, well-connected, professional family. The structured idleness of young women of her class included painting lessons, and quite early on one of Morisot's teachers warned her mother of the impending "catastrophe"—her daughter was in danger of taking painting seriously! And so she did. Intelligent, witty, and beautiful, Berthe Morisot applied her considerable energies to becoming the kind of artist she wanted to be, within the restrictions of upper-class family life. Gentle scenes of domestic harmony, women and children in everyday situations—true to the Impressionist ideal of celebrating the here and now—were executed in a daring and revolutionary technique, already fully formed when Morisot was introduced to Manet in 1868. The serenity of the subject matter almost obscures the courage and ruthlessness of the painting.

Both of these qualities sustained Morisot throughout her career. In spite of a succession of admirers, marriage seemed out of the question for a serious woman painter. Her sister Edma had given up painting after *her* marriage. But when, at the age of thirty-three, Berthe wed Manet's brother, Eugène, she enjoyed the support of a sensitive and loyal partner and the freedom of a married woman with an establishment of her own. Paintings of domestic life (the maid mixing a sauce in the family dining room, husband and daughter playing together in the garden), scenes in the parks and gardens of Neuilly, and landscapes done on holidays in Brittany and Normandy, were shown in all but one of the Impressionist exhibitions.

It is unlikely that Morisot had either the time or the inclination to enjoy pottering in the kitchen like Toulouse-Lautrec, the true aristocrat, but she certainly organized elegant Thursday dinners, where guests praised her "Mexican Rice" and chicken with dates. Her daughter, Julie's, journal mentions some of the regional dishes they enjoyed on holiday—*crêpes* in Brittany and delicious *Moules Bordelaises* in Angoulême. "Exquisite" is a word Julie often uses to describe the food—such as the elegant little cakes provided by Mallarmé for a picnic expedition.

A standing arrangement to dine with friends on the last Friday in the month once resulted in a happy confusion. The Morisot family got the date wrong and arrived in full force to find their hosts settling down to a bowl of soup over the fire. Taking advantage of the diversion, the cats devoured the soup.

Then Mallarmé arrived, all dressed up, saying: "I'm not late, am I?"

"Only a week early."

They all stayed to dinner anyway. The journal does not describe the soup they never ate, but it might well have been the traditional *Potage Bonne Femme*.

Mexican Rice

1½ cups risotto rice, Avorio or Arborio
3 cups stock
1 large onion
1 lb. (500 g) tomatoes
2 cloves garlic, chopped
Salt
Avocadoes, fresh, hot chilies, and coriander leaves for garnish
Olive oil (see page 91)

Chop the onion coarsely and liquidize it with the tomato and garlic. Fry the resultant purée in the olive oil until the "raw onion" smell disappears. Add the rice and cook for five minutes, then pour in the stock. Add salt to taste and cook, covered for twenty minutes on a low heat, by which time the rice should have absorbed the liquid. Decorate with avocado slices, hot chilies, and coriander leaves.

Tuiles

2 egg whites
4 oz. (125 g) flaked almonds
4 oz. (125 g) icing sugar
1 oz. (30 g) ground almonds
1 oz. (30 g) flour
1 oz. (30 g) butter
Salt

Beat the egg whites lightly. Soften the butter and mix with the flour, almonds, sugar, and salt. Mix with the egg whites. Drop spoonfuls onto a greased baking tray and cook in a moderate oven for 15 minutes. Roll each cookie around a bottle or rolling pin to give it a curved shape and leave to cool.

Marie Bracquemond, Tea Time, *1880. Musée du Petit Palais, Paris.*

Moules Bordelaises

2 lbs. (1 kg) mussels
2 glasses dry white wine
1 cup fresh breadcrumbs (see page 90)
1 lb. (500 g) tasty fresh tomatoes
1/2 cup olive oil (see page 91)
2 cloves garlic, chopped
1/2 cup chopped parsley
Salt and pepper

Chop the tomatoes coarsely and cook them rapidly in the olive oil to evaporate the juices. Do not overcook.

Scrub the mussels clean in running water. Cook them in a covered pan with the wine and garlic for a few minutes, until they open. Take the mussels out of their shells and put on one side. Strain the juices through muslin to get rid of the sand. Add the liquid to the tomato sauce, tip in the breadcrumbs and simmer gently until the sauce thickens. Add the mussels and warm through, but do not cook them any more. Serve hot or at room temperature, sprinkled with the parsley.

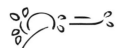

Potage Bonne Femme

A selection of chopped vegetables simmered in water, sieved or puréed, and enriched with butter and cream. The traditional recipe specifies a combination of potatoes, carrots, and leeks seasoned with chervil and parsley, but this makes a nice variation:

2 medium potatoes
2 parsnips
2 leeks
1 thick slice French bread or *Ciabatta* (see page 90)
1 knob of butter
1 cup heavy cream
Grated Gruyère cheese, or Parmesan
Garlic and bay leaf
Parsley and chives
Salt and pepper
1 pint (600 ml) water or stock

Chop the vegetables coarsely and simmer with the bread in the water with garlic to taste and a bay leaf. After half an hour, remove the bay leaf and liquidize. Stir in the butter and cream and re-heat gently. Season with salt and freshly ground black pepper and add the cheese and chopped herbs.

Henri le Sidaner, Lunch Table out of Doors, *(detail). Private Collection.*

Claude Monet, The Lunch, *1868. Städelsches Kunstinstitut, Frankfurt.*

Claude Monet
Eats at Home

Normandy Pheasant

Monet's dire financial problems were, to some extent, self-inflicted. All his life he aspired to standards of living well above his means. The modest rented house in Argenteuil figures in his paintings of the 1870s as a spacious mansion, with lavish flower gardens, and the long-suffering Camille floating, exquisitely dressed, in the rôle of a woman-who-does-not-work. She must have put in considerable efforts behind the scenes to placate creditors and arrange for comfortable bourgeois lunches like the one opposite: *œufs mollets*, lamb cutlets, and potatoes, a decent wine and a nice fresh salad, dressed at the last minute at table, in that serious French ritual: dissolving a little salt in wine vinegar in a serving spoon; sprinkling it over the salad; carefully measuring the olive oil in the same spoon—a proportion of three to one—pouring it over the bowl, and stirring thoroughly. Monet was to do this in later life, when prosperity had actually caught up with him, and guests at Giverny used to blench at the vast quantities of black pepper which he ground over the salads.

Monet loved his domestic life and took great pleasure in his small son and in his garden, buying large blue and white Chinese jars and filling them with scarlet geraniums. He painted young Jean at mealtimes, eagerly banging spoon on plate, or playing contentedly with his toys. The picture of the remains of a summer lunch in the garden at Argenteuil (on page 66) catches the evanescent moment of calm and luxury at the end of a meal out of doors, giving not a hint of the surrounding suburban villas and nearby railroad station, the unpaid laundry bills, and the tangle of personal and financial misfortunes looming in the background.

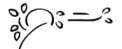

Normandy Pheasant

1 nice plump pheasant
4 good flavored apples, Coxes or Reinettes, cored, unpeeled
   and quartered
2 tablespoons butter
2 bay leaves
Garlic to taste
Salt and pepper
1 cup heavy cream or crème fraîche (see page 91)
1 wineglass Calvados

Brown the pheasant, apples, and garlic in the butter in a
heavy iron casserole. Add the bay leaves. Pour over the
Calvados and set alight. Have the casserole lid ready to clamp
on to douse the flames if necessary. Cook in a moderate oven
for an hour, or until the pheasant is tender.

Take the pheasant out of the pot and carve it. Keep the
pieces warm. Skim any surplus fat from the pan and stir in
the cream to make a rough sauce in which the pieces of apple
have not entirely disintegrated. Put the pheasant joints back
in the pan and warm through.

This recipe is good made with quinces. Whisky can be used
instead of Calvados.

Claude Monet, Still Life with Pheasants and Plovers, *1879. The Minneapolis Institute of Arts.*

Marie Bracquemond, Under the Lamp, *1887. The Art Institute of Chicago, Collection Mr. and Mrs. Potter Palmer.*

Marie Bracquemond
Entertains the Sisleys

Bœuf Bourguignon

"He opens my eyes and makes me see better," said Marie Bracquemond (1841-1916) of Monet. Her own paintings were as innovatory and accomplished as any of the Impressionists but, like her contemporaries, Mary Cassatt, Berthe Morisot, and Eva Gonzalès, she worked within the stifling restrictions of conventional middle class life. Domestic scenes, interiors, ladies of leisure taking tea in the garden, and "mother and child" themes were the terrain on which these intrepid women broke new ground as courageously as their menfolk did in the bars and public places.

Recording the fleeting moment, the play of light on familiar domestic objects, was an indoor as well as an outdoor challenge. Bracquemond's painting of a modest family meal, with guests Alfred Sisley (1839/40-99) and his wife about to help themselves from a fragrant soup or *pot-au-feu*, under the soft glow of the oil lamp, is one of the happiest evocations of domestic life in Impressionist art.

Eventually Bracquemond appears to have sacrificed her art for domestic tranquility, abandoning the painting of which her husband so much disapproved, in spite of encouragement from her sister and son.

The Sisleys also enjoyed modest family dinners with Monet and Camille in an unpretentious setting, typically French in the inclusion of baby Jean in his high chair, learning at a tender age to appreciate the pleasures of the table.

Traditional domestic cooking was a skill handed on from mother to daughter—very different from that of the smart restaurants of Paris and the fashionable holiday resorts of Normandy and, later, the south of France. Both styles, however, had the same strict adherence to rules and conventions. This is difficult for us to appreciate today, when the innovations and fantasies of a generation of brilliant young chefs have dissolved the bonds of conventional wisdom to such an extent that it has provoked a renaissance of *Cuisine Bonne-Maman* and a return to the gently burbling, slow-cooked stews and flour-based sauces of their forebears.

43

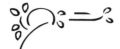

Bœuf Bourguignon

1¹/₂ lbs. (750 g) top round of beef, or a mixture of flank and
    shank, cut into 1-inch (25-mm) cubes.
¹/₄ lb. (125 g) fat streaky bacon, cut into small pieces
¹/₄ lb. (125 g) bacon or ham rind (trimmings from *prosciutto*
    crudo are ideal here), sliced (see page 90)
1 lb. (500 g) onions, chopped
Garlic to taste
¹/₂ bottle good red Burgundy
Bay leaves, thyme, and seasonings to taste
1 tablespoon flour (see page 91)
¹/₂ cup butter

Fry the bacon in a little of the butter. When the fat runs out
add the meat and brown the pieces on all sides. Add the
onions and garlic cloves and brown them a little. Put in the
bay leaves, thyme, freshly ground pepper, and the wine. Cover
the pot and simmer on a low heat for three hours.

    Now taste for salt, there may have been enough in the
bacon. Mash the flour and remaining butter and drop small bits
of this into the juices and stir gently until the sauce thickens.

    A glass of cognac stirred in at this point and simmered for
a few minutes makes a nice finishing touch.

    It is hardly worth bothering to make this dish with
inferior meat, but you can use the less expensive cuts of good
quality beef, stewing venison, or shoulder of wild boar.

Claude Monet, Dinner at Sisley's, *1867. Collection E. G. Bührle, Zurich.*

Mary Cassatt, Feeding the Ducks, *c. 1894. An enthusiasm for the arts of Japan was shared by many of the Impressionists. Cassatt wrote enthusiastically to Morisot urging her to visit the exhibition of Japanese prints at the École des Beaux-Arts in 1890, and herself produced a series of lithographs influenced by their asymmetric compositions. Terra Museum of American Art, Chicago.*

Mary Cassatt
Feeds the Ducks

Confit de Canard
Chilled Summer Soup

Even the independent and single-minded American, Mary Cassatt (1844-1926), who settled with her parents and sister Lydia in Paris in the 1870s, was not free to pursue many of the outdoor subjects painted by men. The lakes and gardens in the Bois de Boulogne, however, were a safe and convenient location, and both Cassatt and Morisot produced lyrical images of mothers and children feeding the ducks or idling on the water.

Duck is a difficult subject for summer cooking, its richness a bit overpowering for some. A *confit de canard* has the advantage of parting joints of duck from their surrounding fat, leaving succulent flesh which can be gently re-heated and served with a light, crisp salad or a cold purée of lentils or turnips.

The French know how to handle the intense heat of summer. Doors and windows are closed to trap the cool night air, while shutters and blinds keep the sun off walls and windows. A meal indoors in a dim, cool dining room, with light, fragrant food and chilled wine is a civilized alternative to an outdoor picnic.

The chilled soup was one of Édouard de Pomiane's offerings in his celebrated radio programmes of the 1920s and 30s. His combination of charm, verbal dexterity, and *chutzpah* conveyed a distillation of classic cuisine and fresh, new ideas to listeners in unbelievably short sound bites. They were probably the best food programmes ever.

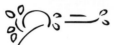

Confit de Canard

This serious way of preserving duck or goose for use throughout the year can be adapted to make ordinary domestic meals.

4 duck legs (thigh and drumstick)
2 teaspoons of salt for every pound of duck
Garlic, thyme, peppercorns, and bay leaves to taste
1 cup rendered duck fat or good quality lard (see page 90 and 91)

Marinate the duck in the aromatics for a day or more. Melt the duck fat in a heavy casserole and add the joints, wiped of their marinade. The fat should cover them completely. Cook on a very low heat until the meat is tender. This will take an hour or two. Let the duck cool in the fat, then put the pieces in storage jars or containers and cover with the strained soft fat. They can be eaten at once, but the flavor of the duck matures with keeping.

Serve the *confit* warm. Fat lovers can wallow in the crisped skin and rich juices, but the aromatic flesh can be separated from the fat and served with a fresh, tart salad or plain boiled lentils for those with less robust constitutions.

Chilled Summer Soup

1 1/2 lbs. (750 g) ripe tomatoes
1 medium-sized cucumber, sliced, grated, or cubed
1 pint (600 ml) water
1 cup heavy cream
1 tablespoon semolina
Fresh herbs: chervil and tarragon, or basil and chives, chopped
Salt and pepper to taste
Garlic if wished

It is not worth even *thinking* about this recipe unless you can get some decent tomatoes. The symmetrical, tasteless red blobs that sit around in our supermarkets can be replaced by different varieties "grown for flavor." Canned ones will not do either.

Liquidize the tomatoes with the water. Sieve for a really smooth effect, or retain the skins and bits for texture. Put in a heavy saucepan and bring to the boil. Slowly stir in the semolina and cook until the soup thickens (about ten minutes). Let it cool. Stir in the cucumber, cream, and chopped herbs, seasoning with garlic, salt, and black pepper to taste. Chill. Serve with croûtons or crusty bread (see pages 90 and 91).

Henri le Sidaner, Tea in the Woods at Gerberoy, *1925. The evanescent presence of fruit, flowers, and wine hovers in the dappled shade, but the food — like the people — seems to play little part in this insubstantial picnic. Private Collection.*

Édouard Vuillard, Toulouse-Lautrec Cooking, *1898. Vuillard painted his friend at Villeneuve-sur-Yonne at the country house of Misia and Thadée Natanson, where they were frequent guests. Lautrec's generosity and* joie de vivre *found ideal expression in cooking, wherever he happened to be. Musée Toulouse-Lautrec, Albi.*

Toulouse-Lautrec
Cooks for "The Happy Few"

Ramereaux aux Olives (Pigeons with Olives)
Homard à l'Américaine
Bacchic Cream
Ricotta with Wine
Little Savory Custards
Ile Flottante

"Ah la vie! La vie!" Henri de Toulouse-Lautrec (1864-1901) would cry, plunging into all the delights and sensations life had to offer with enthusiasm and generosity. Food and drink were foremost among the pleasures he shared with chosen friends. He kept a well-stocked bar in his studio to mix for his visitors cocktails appropriate to the paintings displayed for their enjoyment. There were regular Friday dinners when menus and shopping lists were plotted and schemed in advance, with fine wines and expensive chickens stuffed with truffles sent down from his family estates in Albi.

A special recipe discovered in an old-fashioned eating house in the Rue de Bourgogne, was *Ramereaux aux Olives* (young woodpigeons with olives). It was prepared for the band of loyal friends who formed a protective circle when the notoriety created by Lautrec's studies of brothel scenes became intrusive. Behind closed doors, "The Happy Few" enjoyed this delectable dish and shielded their friend from the pressures and publicity. It became a symbol of a state of mind, a special token of friendship.

Something of the spirit of the Impressionist picnic inspired the occasion when Lautrec abandoned the well-appointed kitchen of his friend, the antiquarian book dealer Georges Henri-Manuel, and insisted on cooking *Homard à l'Américaine* on a portable stove in his host's elegant book-lined salon. This almost unforgivable prank was redeemed by the fact that the lobster was exquisite, and prepared without a single splash or splutter.

There came a time when the indulgence in good things took its toll, and his family and friends attempted to persuade Lautrec to mend his ways and think about adopting a less punishing diet. He replied with this elegant invitation to the opening of his new studio, where, amid the Japanese prints and textiles, a table laden with milk products, in the latest fashion—cheeses, little cakes, bowls of whipped cream, and pots of yoghurt—almost obscured the carefully concealed cocktail cabinet, which continued to refresh "The Happy Few" in the style to which they were accustomed.

Ramereaux aux Olives— (Pigeons with Olives)

For four people:
4 young woodpigeons (tame pigeons or squabs, can be used,
　with shorter cooking time)
6 shallots, chopped
1/4 cup each of ground beef, veal, and fat pork
4 oz. (125 g) fatty unsmoked bacon or *pancetta* (see page 90)
Salt, pepper, nutmeg, herbs (sage, rosemary, and bay leaves)
1 tablespoon butter
1 glass of Cognac
1 cup of pitted green olives
2 cups good, home-made stock
1 tablespoon flour (see page 91)

Mix the ground meats with salt, pepper and nutmeg.
(Toulouse-Lautrec used truffles as well; do so if you can.)
Stuff the birds with this. Fry the shallots and bacon in the
butter, add the flour and cook for a minute, pour in the stock
and stir well. Add the birds, breast down, and herbs. Cook,
covered, at a gentle simmer until the birds are tender. Young
pigeons will take about an hour, elderly ones a great deal
longer. Squabs will be done in an hour or three quarters of an
hour.

Now put into the pot the green olives, Cognac, and a generous amount of freshly ground black pepper and simmer, uncovered, to allow the sauce to concentrate.

Serve with plain boiled rice or mashed potatoes.

Homard à l'Américaine

1 lobster
1 clove garlic, chopped
2 tablespoons olive oil (see page 91)
1 small glass brandy
1 medium onion, chopped
3 medium tomatoes, chopped
Fresh thyme, parsley, and fennel, chopped
1 bay leaf
1 glass dry white wine
1 tablespoon butter

Get your fishmonger to cut a humanely killed lobster into serving pieces, reserving the coral and tomalley.

Heat the oil in a heavy pan and cook the lobster pieces with the garlic until they turn red. Pour in the brandy and set alight. When the flames have died down take out the lobster and keep to one side. Cook the onion in the juices in the pan until soft, then add the tomatoes, wine, and lobster and cook, uncovered, until the lobster is done (10 to 15 minutes). Mash the coral and tomalley with the butter and stir into the juices. Warm through without boiling.

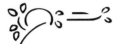

Bacchic Cream

This innocent looking custard, from Geraldene Holt's *French Country Kitchen*, would have been a nice addition to Toulouse-Lautrec's Milk Bar.

4 egg yolks
½ pint (300 ml) sweet white wine, Montbazillac or
    Beaumes de Venise
Sugar to taste, depending on the sweetness of the wine
Lemon zest or cinnamon

Warm the wine in an enamel pan with the lemon or cinnamon. Let it infuse a while. Beat the egg yolks in a bowl and stir in the wine. Pour the mixture into little pots or ramekins, place them in a baking tin with water in it and cook in a moderate oven until set.

Ricotta with Wine

This is less rich than the above, more suitable for penitent gourmets.

8 oz. (250 g) ricotta or fromage blanc
2 oz. (60 g) sugar
1 glass assertive dry white wine
A little bitter orange zest (see page 90)

Whiz everything together in a blender or food processor. Chill. Serve with the *tuiles* on page 35.

Henri de Toulouse-Lautrec, Invitation. *This ironic little invitation
to take a cup of milk to celebrate the opening of his new studio
contains a pun on the alleged diuretic effects of milk in the
inclusion of a magpie—"Pie", as in "Pi-Pi"!*

Little Savory Custards

Mix 4 eggs with 1 cup of heavy cream, 1 cup of grated
Gruyère, ½ cup chopped tarragon and chives, a pinch of salt,
and a little freshly ground black pepper and nutmeg. Bake in
little ramekins or in a bain-marie (see page 90) until just set.

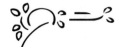

Ile Flottante

This variation on a familiar theme was written in faded purple ink on a folded scrap of paper in *La Cuisine de Rose-Marie*, a turn-of-the-century cookbook handed down to me by a frugal French family from the Cévennes. The instructions insist that large quantities are made to allow for lavish second helpings.

4 eggs
1 cup heavy cream
1 cup milk
1 vanilla pod
1 cup of pulverized pralines (see page 92)
1 cup sugar

Beat the whites of the egg until firm. Add the praline mixture and half the sugar, beating all the time. Cook this meringue mixture in a well-buttered bowl, sitting in a bain-marie, (see page 90) in a moderate oven for 45 minutes.

Meanwhile, make a custard with the egg yolks, milk, cream, and remaining sugar, flavored with the vanilla pod. Let both the pudding and the custard cool. Turn the meringue out into a decorative bowl and serve surrounded by the custard and sprinkled with a little praline powder.

Martha Walter, At the Teashop, *1910. Terra Museum of American Art, Chicago.*

Paul Cézanne
Takes His Pleasures
Seriously

Salade Niçoise
Mangoes with Crème Chantilly
Crème Chantilly

The shimmering evocation of a meal out of doors is less important to Paul Cézanne (1839-1906) than the reworking of a classical theme, the *fête champêtre*, bringing the gods and godesses of Arcadia down to earth with a bump. Cézanne's passionate nature made him an impossible friend and companion, but his honesty, in life as in art, towers above everything he did. "At least he knows how to buy olives ... ." was his assessment of an unpopular brother-in-law.

Paul Cézanne, Déjeuner sur l'Herbe, *1872-82. Musée de Picardie, Amiens.*

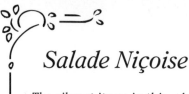

Salade Niçoise

The vibrant items in this salad are the anchovies, olives, and tuna. Whatever else you add should provide a foil—the blandness of the eggs, potatoes, and beans and the crisp bite of the lettuce and pepper provide contrasting textures. You can try these variations, but not all at once: omit all red items to create a harmony of greens, off-white, and black or use radishes, red and yellow peppers, tomatoes, and red lettuce and go easy on the greenery.

½ lb. (250 g) small green beans, cooked and cut into 1 inch (25-mm) lengths
4 hard-boiled eggs, peeled and halved
12 cured anchovy fillets, desalted and cleaned
12 large black olives
1 cup canned tuna fish
1 red onion, sliced
1 lettuce heart
Parsley or basil, chopped
1 green pepper, chopped
2 tasty tomatoes, cut into chunks
Garlic, salt, and freshly ground black pepper to taste
Extra virgin olive oil (see page 91)

Mix everything together with the oil. Don't strain for a sophisticated decorative arrangement; this is hearty peasant food—it makes its own pattern. Those who like the bite of a good wine vinegar can add a few drops separately.

Paul Gauguin, Still Life with Mangoes. *Private Collection.*

Mangoes with Crème Chantilly

Mangoes are so impossible to eat with any degree of elegance in a social situation, that it is a kindness to guests or picnicers to get the flesh off the stone well in advance. If the fruit is perfectly ripe and full of flavor, it does not need any extra attention, but you could put cubes of mango in a glass bowl with light rum and sugar, chill, and serve with *Crème Chantilly*.

Crème Chantilly

Whip 1/2 pint (300 ml) heavy cream with a wire whisk in a chilled bowl. Doing this by hand incorporates more air and makes it lighter. Flavor with vanilla sugar or an appropriate liqueur.

61

Pierre Bonnard, The Table, *1925. The Tate Gallery, London.*

Pierre Bonnard's Indoor Picnic

Tarte aux Fraises
Strawberry Salad
Pain Perdu
Tomato Sauce

"Rather low in the ceiling" was the irreverent way in which Pierre Bonnard's (1867-1947) young contemporaries, the Nabis (see page 91-92), spoke of the respected Impressionists, with their determination to record the world in light and color rather than intellectualize about it. Bonnard himself did not care to get too caught up in theories, but his paintings are more complex than a simple recording of impressions and sensations. Meals, or the remains of them, figure in many of his paintings, but they do not convey to us any precise sense of a planned menu or cuisine. We wonder if the ethereal Marthe, emerging after hours in her irridescent bathtub, ever set foot in a kitchen. Food appears to find its way onto Bonnard's tables in mysterious conjunctions with little black dogs, importunate small cats, patterned surfaces, and intimations of fragrance and aromas; all in strange and carefully wrought perspectives.

Bonnard's light desserts and bowls of fruit, cakes, pastries, and creams look more like picnic food than the fixed certainties of Monet's household, where he was often a guest. His own house at Le Canet in the south was very different from the patriarchal establishment at Giverny. He furnished it with country furniture and cane chairs. Bright red felt covered the dining table and the warm smells of the Midi drifted in from the garden, to mingle with the enigmatic odors of Bonnard's mysterious kitchen.

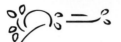

Tarte aux Fraises

The pastry:
8 oz. (250 g) flour
4 oz. (125 g) butter cut into small pieces
4 oz. (125 g) vanilla sugar
1 egg, a pinch of salt

Beat the egg, salt, and sugar together. Add the flour and mix until the paste feels sandy, then add the butter and knead rapidly. Roll out and line a 9-inch (22.5-cm) flan dish. Blind bake until golden.

The filling
1 lb. (500 g) strawberries, halved
2 tablespoons red-currant jelly
1 tablespoon sugar

Put a layer of strawberries in the pastry case. Melt the sugar in the jelly and bring to the boil. Cool until blood heat and pour over the fruit. Eat cold.

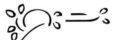

Strawberry Salad

Boredom can easily set in with those large, bloated strawberries—sometimes a bit jaded by their long journey in a refrigerated lorry or freight container—which are available almost all the year round now.

They can, however, gain a new lease of life in a salad, with sliced cucumber, seasoned with salt and freshly ground black pepper, a little chopped garlic, some Balsamic vinegar (see page 90), hazelnut oil, and fresh mint leaves.

This salad goes well with cold cooked ham, cold roast beef or lamb, roast chicken, or a country pâté.

Pain Perdu

4 slices good white bread, crusts removed (see page 90)
1½ cups milk
2 eggs
Vanilla sugar
Cinnamon, freshly ground
Butter

Cut the slices of bread into fingers. Soak them in the eggs beaten with the milk. Melt the butter in a solid frying pan and fry the bread gently in it. Dust with sugar and cinnamon. Eat hot.

You can make this into a savory treat by sprinkling with freshly grated Parmesan and nutmeg. Since all children seem to like tomato sauce, give them a dollop of a good home-made one to dunk the bread fingers in.

Tomato Sauce

Coarsely chop 4 ripe tomatoes and cook them in good olive oil (see page 91) with a little garlic and paprika. Salt to taste. Add a pinch of sugar if the tomatoes are a bit tart.

Pierre Bonnard. The Children's Lunch, *Musée des Beaux Arts, Nancy.*

Claude Monet, Le Déjeuner, *1872-74. Painted some time before Monet's move to Giverny, this epitomizes the pleasures of lunch out of doors, in a well-tended garden, with young Jean placidly at play in the shade and elegant guests swishing over the gravel paths. Musée d'Orsay, Paris.*

The Patriarch
At Giverny

Baked Red Mullet
Whistler's Mother's Pudding
Roast Beef

From the brusque young artist who scarpered without paying his hotel bill in Normandy in the 1860s into the responsible, somewhat tyrannical sage of Giverny is but a short step. In 1868 Monet found himself at his lowest ebb, financially and emotionally. His patron, Ernest Hoschedé, had collapsed into bankruptcy, leaving his wife, Alice, and their children, without support. The Hoschedé family joined forces with Monet and his ailing wife, Camille, already debilitated by the birth of their second child and demoralized by her husband's affair with Alice Hoschedé.

Somehow Monet, with the energetic assistance of Alice, managed to pick up some of the pieces and hold together this large family, his own two children and six of hers, first at Vétheuil, after Camille's death, and later, further up the river at the village of Giverny, where they moved—the whole household packed onto barges. There they set about creating the way of life which subsequent hordes of sightseers cannot quite obliterate, a garden hewn from swamp and water-meadows, a house full of light clear colors, and the calm enjoyment of hard-won domestic serenity.

Monet's bedroom has windows looking towards the south and west, from which the day's weather could be predicted, and the day's work planned. His day began at five in the morning, with time spent in the kitchen garden planning the week's menus, followed by time in the flower gardens where—with the help of children and later, gardeners—the vistas of water, flowers, and pink-washed walls would emerge. Then, on the dot, and at the sound of a peremptory bell, family and guests would gather for the early lunch, carved and served by the master himself, enjoyed and eaten without loitering, for the afternoon light was too good to miss.

Julie Manet, Berthe Morisot's daughter, was a bit fazed by Monet's table manners (soup all over the majestic beard) but loved the paintings, especially the series of Rouen cathedral, which made her think of dollops of strawberry ice-cream.

Claude Monet, Fish, *c. 1870. Fogg Art Musuem, Harvard University.*

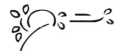

Baked Red Mullet

4 red mullet, with or without their livers, according to taste
2 cloves garlic, peeled and chopped
1/2 cup chopped parsley
1/2 cup chopped, stoned black olives
1 teaspoon of grated lemon zest
The juice of 1 lemon
Salt and pepper
4 medium-sized tomatoes
Basil leaves
8 whole black olives
Olive oil (see page 91)

Mix the garlic, parsley, olives and lemon together with salt and
freshly ground black pepper. Stuff the cleaned mullet with this
and let them absorb the flavors in a cool place for an hour or so.

Brush the fish with olive oil and bake in a hot oven for 10
to 15 minutes.

Meanwhile, cook the chopped tomatoes in the olive oil
quickly to concentrate the juices. Salt to taste and add the
torn up basil leaves and any juices from the mullet. Pour over
the fish and serve garnished with the olives. This is good
eaten hot or at room temperature.

James Abbott McNeill Whistler (1843-1903), on one of his visits to Giverny, may have been reminded of one of his mother's exquisite puddings, her very American version of *Iles Flottantes*. Whistler's love of good food matched that of his friends Maurice Joyant and Toulouse-Lautrec, but the pretentious dinner he offered them at the Café Royal in London was a flop. The two friends plotted a return match at the Criterion, where a whole side of beef was roasted and carved to Lautrec's precise instructions, and Whistler was forced to concede defeat on his own ground. Monet, on *his* trips to London, had less happy experiences, and wrote home to Alice complaining of the awful food.

Whistler's Mother's Pudding

The whites of 3 eggs
1 cup red-currant jelly
2 cups heavy cream
1 tablespoon sugar
1 tablespoon rosewater
Milk

Whip the cream with the sugar until thick and smooth. Put it in a shallow bowl and spread it flat.

Whip the egg whites until stiff, gradually adding the red-currant jelly and rosewater. Poach spoonfulls of this meringue in a shallow pan of milk. Let them cool, then serve on the bed of whipped cream.

The classic version uses the yolks of the eggs to make a custard in which the pink blobs of meringue will float, like so many waterlilies.

Claude Monet, Rouen Cathedral, Façade, *1892-94. In the 1880s Monet, never one for theorizing, set about making "series" paintings of a variety of subjects, which have prompted much theorizing from others. Museum of Fine Arts, Boston, Juliana Cheney Edwards Collection.*

Above: William Orpen, The Cook. *"All good cooks drink,"
proclaimed Whistler, whose recommendation of a less than sober
cook/housekeeper admitted that "so good was her cooking that
possibly more indulgence may have been shown to her than
another with her faults would have received ...". A fitting tribute
to his own culinary prowess and that of many of his friends. The
chef portrayed here, however is a reminder of the fine food that
could be enjoyed in the clubs and restaurants of London visited
by Lautrec and Maurice Joyant on their frequent visits to British
dealers and galleries. Royal Academy of Arts, London. Right:
Claude Monet,* Joint of Beef, *c. 1864. Musée d'Orsay, Paris.*

Roast Beef

The myth that it's no good roasting a small joint of beef, that somehow only the vast Victorian family Sunday lunch can ever know the full glory of the dark, flavorful outer portions and the meltingly tender pinkness of the inside, is one that the nuclear family—all 2.75 members of it—is well on the way to exploding.

For four people take a 2$^{1}/_{2}$ to 3-lb. (1.25 - 1.5 kg) joint of sirloin on the bone. Flavor it with garlic or rosemary (or whatever you please). Put it on a rack in a roasting tin and cook in a hot oven for about 45 minutes. The roasting time will depend upon the behavior of your oven, the tastes of your family, and the condition of the beef. One thing is certain— you are on your own, you and the best butcher you can find. Ask his advice, pay what it costs, and don't even *think* of serving roast beef unless you can get a properly hung piece of really first-class meat.

Some advise coating the joint with chestnut flour and putting a glass of red wine in the roasting pan to help with the gravy.

Camille Pissarro, Kitchen garden at l'Hermitage. *The awfulness of cabbage in English cooking blinds many of us to the honorable rôle it has in the cuisine of France. Lightly cooked and dressed with butter and herbs, slow cooked with a subtle range of aromatics, or stuffed in various ways, the cabbage is one of the mainstays of traditional French food. National Gallery of Scotland, Edinburgh.*

Camille Pissarro
In the Cabbage Patch

Chou Farci (Stuffed Cabbage)

Camille Pissarro (1830-1903) was the only one of the Impressionists to paint the countryside with any sympathy for the people who shaped it and lived in it. His gardens were old-fashioned village plots, with pot herbs, flowers, and vegetables in a utilitarian rather than picturesque profusion. Very different from Monet's massed herbaceous borders—a city-dweller's view of nature—the apotheosis of the suburban garden. Pissarro's radical political views made him more concerned about the living conditions of the peasants he painted. He never quite forgave Jean-François Millet (1814-75) for using them as romantic ingredients in his landscapes.

The laconic Édouard de Pomiane (see page 47) allowed himself the luxury of a purple patch at the beginning of his memorable cabbage broadcast:

"The Feast of All Saints has expired and the shaggy crysanthemums fade slowly on its grave, lit up by the dying fall of the last rays of the autumnal sun. The somber market stalls have lost their glowing vegetables, only the odd crimson carrot glows alongside the huge, rotund forms of the palid green and white cabbages." Winter does have its compensations....

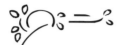

Chou Farci (Stuffed Cabbage)

1 firm cabbage
4 oz. (125 g) cooked ham
8 oz. (250 g) fatty pork
4 oz. (125 g) bacon or *pancetta* (see page 90)
8 rashers streaky bacon
8 oz. (250g) cooked chestnuts
4 cloves garlic, peeled and chopped
1 cup chopped parsley
¹/₂ cup fresh breadcrumbs
¹/₂ teaspoon thyme
Salt and pepper
Butter

Trim the cabbage of its coarse outer leaves and blanch for 5 minutes in a pot of boiling water, then put it in a bowl of cold water.

Chop the ham, pork, and *pancetta* and mix with the egg, chestnuts, breadcrumbs, garlic, thyme, and parsley. Season with salt and pepper. Gently prize the leaves of the cabbage apart and stuff some of the mixture between each one. Bash the unwieldy thing back into shape and tie it up with string. Wrap it in the rashers of bacon and secure them with more string. Put the cabbage in a deep ovenproof pot and daub butter all over it. Bake in a moderate oven for 1¹/₂ hours or more, basting with dry white wine and the cooking juices. Cover with foil if it looks like drying out. Carve in its dish and eat hot.

Alternatively the stuffed cabbage can be simmered in stock. When done, remove from the cooking liquid, which can be thickened with *beurre manié* and served as a sauce with the carved cabbage.

Camille Pissarro, The Pork Butcher. *Pissarro was one of the few Impressionist painters who painted earlier stages in the process which culminated in the laden table. The profusion of local produce in markets and gardens—cheeses, pâtés, hams, cooked and cured meats—are still one of the glories of French provincial life. The Tate Gallery, London.*

Édouard Vuillard, Madame Vuillard in an Interior, *c. 1895.*
Vuillard's Muse in her kingdom, the kitchen. Private Collection.

Édouard Vuillard
The Perfect Guest
& His Muse

Green Navarin
Les Crêpes Frisées de Tante Jeanette
(Lacy Pancakes)

The young Édouard Vuillard (1868-1940) and his friend Bonnard carried on the tradition of the *flâneur*—the debonair man about town, frequenter of smart salons and avant-garde print studios, the cafés and music halls of Montmartre, as well as the studios of a new generation of adventurous and cerebral artists and writers, the Nabis (see page 91-92). Easy enough for Bonnard, whose wealthy professional family supported him in his half-hearted law studies and subsequent career as a painter. Vuillard, from a modest, artisan background, relied heavily on the financial support and sound business sense of his mother, a dressmaker and corsetière. She kept house for him and many of his most serene paintings show her sewing, or sitting placidly by an open window, amid the peaceful clutter of a Parisian bourgeois apartment.

Meal-times reveal a different aspect of Vuillard family life, a claustrophobic sense of pressures and cross-currents, stifling constraints, and pent-up grudges. Very different from the relaxed, open air meals Vuillard enjoyed as house guest of his friends and patrons Misia and Thadée Natanson, and in country houses in Normandy and the countryside around Paris. The food must have been a contrast too, his mother's sound family dishes and the more modern, chic cuisine of his cosmopolitan friends—from *La Véritable Cuisine de Famille* of "Tante Marie" to Escoffier's *Le Guide Culinaire*.

His sister, so repressed in her mother's house, married Vuillard's friend, the artist Ker-Xavier Roussel. Later paintings of family scenes with her children suggest a happier relationship with the formidable old matriarch.

Vuillard was the perfect guest, a good listener, and a kind and sympathetic companion, perhaps because of his capacity to observe, aloof, the different households in which he never really belonged.

Édouard Vuillard, The Meal, *c. 1895. An informal meal with his avant-garde friends, fashionable blue and white china, local wine from a jug drunk out of stout tumblers—all very different from the conventions of Vuillard's solid middle class background. Yale University Art Gallery, New Haven, Katharine Ordway Collection.*

Green Navarin

The knack with this dish is to add the different ingredients at different points in the cooking so that they are all done at the same time. It all depends on the age and condition of the vegetables you choose, so cooking times here are approximate.

For six people:
2-lb. (1-kg) leg of spring lamb, cut into 1-inch (25-mm) cubes, with the fat removed
2 oz. (60 g) unsmoked fatty bacon or *pancetta*, cubed (see page 90)
1 large onion, finely chopped
2 bay leaves and a sprig of rosemary
Garlic to taste
8 medium sized new potatoes
2 lbs. (1 kg) broad beans
2 lbs. (1 kg) young peas
1 cup chopped parsley
1 cup chopped fresh herbs, including: mint, chervil, lemon balm, and basil
1 glass white wine
Flour and a knob of butter (see page 91)
Salt and pepper

Put the lamb in a large casserole with the bacon, onions, bay leaves, rosemary, garlic, wine, and enough water to cover. By the time all the ingredients have cooked there should be only a small amount of aromatic liquid, so add water as you go along rather than too much at the start.

Simmer until the lamb is three quarters done. Add the potatoes and cook for 10 minutes. Then put in the broad beans and cook for 5 minutes. Tip in the peas and cook for 10 minutes more. Test for seasoning and add salt and pepper to taste.

Mash the butter with 1 tablespoon of flour and drop little bits into the casserole to thicken the juices. Now add the green herbs and stir, but from now on no more cooking or the fresh green of the herbs will fade. The saltpeter in the bacon will have given the lamb a pink tinge, which looks charming with the greenery.

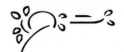

Les Crêpes Frisées de Tante Jeanette (Lacy Pancakes)

2 eggs
1 cup flour
1 cup milk
Salt
Vanilla sugar
Brandy
Grape seed oil (see page 91)

Beat the eggs with enough flour and milk to make a light batter. Salt to taste. Leave to rest for an hour or so. Beat in a glass of brandy. Lightly oil a heavy frying pan and heat. Dribble the batter to make patterns over the base of the pan, with plenty of holes which will crisp round the edges as the pancake cooks. Toss or flip and cook the other side. Serve all hot and crisp, sprinkled with sugar and lemon juice.

Overleaf: Édouard Vuillard, The Salad Bowl, *c. 1887-88. Musée d'Orsay, Paris. Right: Édouard Vuillard,* The Meal, *c. 1899. Philadelphia Museum of Art, Gift of Henry P. McIlhenny.*

André Dunoyer de Segonzac, Flowers and Peaches, *Private Collection.*

Gertrude Stein
Goes For a Drive

Alice B. Toklas's Picnic Sandwiches
Ham & Fennel

Sometimes Gertrude Stein (1874-1946) and her companion Alice B. Toklas traveled for the scenery and the weather, sometimes for the food. Their picnics were prepared with an assured hand.

Alice B. Toklas was a good person to have on hand in a crisis. When San Francisco caught fire after the 1906 earthquake, she and her father rushed out and bought two large hams and four hundred cigarettes, thus enabling them to dispense hospitality and refreshment to their friends. Again, in 1940, when German planes were skirmishing over their heads in Bilignin, not far from the French Alps, she and Gertrude Stein hastened to the nearest town and purchased two hams and a large quantity of cigarettes. They cooked the hams in *eau de vie de Marc* which preserved them nicely until the following spring—and they and their friends survived the remaining dark days of the German occupation on vegetables from Alice B. Toklas's well-tended kitchen garden.

Today, the pleasure of cooking a large ham can lead to despair when faced with the bleak vista of endless cold ham salads. Here is a way of using slices of ham in an elegant dish in which the blandness of fennel and cheese complement the rich saltiness of the ham.

Alice B. Toklas's Picnic Sandwiches

1 cup chopped, rare, roast beef
1 teaspoon mustard powder
1 teaspoon chopped shallot
1 tablespoon sun-dried, marinated tomatoes, chopped
1 tablespoon crème fraîche (see page 91)
1 tablespoon chopped parsley
Salt and pepper

Mix well together and use to fill sandwiches or stuff crisp little rolls.

Édouard Manet, The Ham, *c. 1875-78. The Burrell Collection, Glasgow.*

6 slices cooked ham
3 bulbs of fennel
1 cup grated Gruyère cheese
1/2 cup grated Parmesan
1 cup milk
1/2 cup butter
1 tablespoon flour (see page 91)
Salt, pepper, and nutmeg
A few fennel seeds

Trim the fennel, reserving any green fronds. Cut each bulb in half and simmer with the fennel seeds in a little water until soft. Keep the water for the sauce.

Melt the butter and cook the flour in it for a few minutes. Stir in the fennel cooking liquid and the milk to make a smooth sauce. Add half the Parmesan and half the Gruyère.

Season each piece of fennel with freshly ground black pepper, nutmeg, and Parmesan. Roll each piece in a slice of ham and pack into an ovenproof dish. Cover with the sauce. Put bits of butter and the rest of the Gruyère over the sauce and warm through in a hot oven.

Serve garnished with the fennel fronds.

Glossary & Notes

Bacon: *(lard)* when specified in most recipes, should be hard, dry-salted bacon, not the light-cured, watery stuff mostly available. *Pancetta* (the slabs of streaky bacon, not the rolled salami-style pancetta) from Italian stores, is ideal. In slow-cooked stews and casseroles, the rinds should be left on because they impart a smooth quality to the sauce.

Bain-marie: Old-fashioned kitchen ranges had a compartment holding hot water in which pots and pans could be placed to allow for the slow maturing of sauces, and the cooking of fragile custards and creams. Nowadays a double boiler is used, or a bowl sitting over a pan of hot water. When making tricky sauces like Hollandaise or Beurre Blanc, it is helpful to have a basin of cold water handy to cool a container which is in danger of getting too hot and making things curdle.

Balsamic vinegar: is a currently fashionable, aromatic vinegar from the area around Modena in Italy. Commercial versions are so different from the artisanal product—a very expensive, exquisitely flavored, almost syrupy condiment—that it is unfortunate that they share the same name.

Bitter or Seville orange juice: is more acid and flavorful than sweet orange juice. A few drops in a salad are sometimes more appropriate than wine vinegar, or can be added to it. Small scrapings of peel (zest) are a good flavoring in slow-cooked stews.

Bread: used in cooking has to be good. As hard to find in France now as in other countries. Italian style *ciabatta* is better than tasteless *baguettes*. Breadcrumbs for cooking can easily be home made from stale or fresh bread, whizzed up in a blender. The ancient use of bread to thicken sauces and stews is worth reviving, it gives a better flavor and texture than a wrongly handled flour-based thickener. The version of *Soupe Bonne Femme* uses bread cooked with the vegetables until soft and swollen before liquidizing. The flavor and texture are very good.

Crème fraîche: is a slightly fermented thick cream with a sharpness lacking in pasteurized creams.

Croûtons: are little cubes of bread fried in oil, butter, duck or goose fat, with garlic if appropriate, and served to give texture and additional flavor to bland or smooth dishes.

Fat: Since the characteristics of France's different regional cuisines depend on the kind of fat—butter and cream, lard, goose and duck fat, or oil—used in them, it is as well to follow traditional recipes for authenticity, but adapt for health reasons. Olive oil is currently held to be the most beneficial, but goose and duck fat are enjoying a come-back at the moment.

Flâneur: is neither a flan nor a tart, but the name given to the suave, sophisticated man-about-town who personified, in literature and art, the cool, intelligent, detached observer of Parisian life—either strolling elegantly along the boulevards or seated, aloof and ironic, in fashionable bars or side-walk cafés.

Flour: in sauces used to be held in contempt. It can produce a stodgy, gluey result if not allowed to mature in a bain-marie or on a very low heat. The alternative—a drastic reduction of the cooking liquid—can be equally unpleasant. *Beurre manié,* flour mashed up with butter and added at the end of cooking to a stew or casserole in which the juices have slowly diminished, give a shiny, smooth finish. Breadcrumbs (see above) are a pleasant alternative. Rice or potato flour can be used as a substitute for wheat flour.

Nabi: is the Hebrew word for prophet, a name adopted by the group of young artists founded in 1888, which included Vuillard, Bonnard, and Maurice Denis, who explored new developments in graphic design and theories of art, working in the theater and interior decoration, and delighting in richly patterned surfaces and assymetrical composition.

Oil: usually means olive oil. Extra virgin olive oil, with its wide range of flavors and aromas, is good for salads and dishes in which you select a particular oil to enhance the taste of a raw or cooked green vegetable. It is a waste to use it for frying or for recipes where other, heavier flavorings predominate. Use the virtually tasteless grapeseed oil instead.

Polenta: *semoule,* maize flour, of varying degrees of coarseness, boiled with water (stirred constantly) makes a good accompaniment to red meat and chicken dishes. The addition of butter and cheese produces a nutritious dish in its own right, served with tomato sauce.

Praline: is a mixture of roasted almonds and caramelized sugar, usually crushed or powdered, and used as a flavoring for biscuits and desserts.

Sformata: is the Italian version of a soufflé, usually made without beating the egg whites separately. Pre-cooked vegetables are mixed with a béchamel sauce, or breadcrumbs, cheese, eggs, and flavorings and baked in a tin or mould. The French version of this, sometimes without eggs, would be a *tian.*

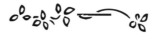

A Note on Quantities: Metric equivalents have been calculated to the nearest round figure, adjusted up or down as appropriate to the nature of the recipe—assuming that most domestic cooks prefer to use their own idiosyncratic rules-of-thumb. We have also assumed that cups, proportionally used, will give adequate guidance in either English or American measures within the context of each recipe.

To cook an ingredient "until tender" depends so much on the size and type of vegetable, fowl, or cut of meat in question, that precise instructions have been avoided where they might be less than helpful.

Acknowledgements

My warmest thanks go to my editor, Treld Pelkey Bicknell, for her enthusiasm and know-how; and to her assistant, Lucinda Pearce-Higgins, for her patience and perseverance with the picture research. Special thanks go to Maggie Black, whose expertise and sound judgement have been invaluable throughout.

The following people have also helped in many ways, with advice, information, and encouragement: John Bartlett, Neville Binet, James Mosley, Carol and Robbie Robson, Alex Saunderson, Joan Stanton, Alexander Sturgis, and Tessa Trethowan of Christie's Images. My thanks to Glynn Pickerill and The R & B Partnership for lending us their skills.

Illustrations

The author and publisher wish to thank the following for permission to reproduce copyright material: Christie's Images for front and back cover and pp. 28-29, 37, 49, 61, 78, and 86; Musée d'Orsay (© R.M.N.) for frontispiece and pp. 8, 10, 66, 73, and 82-83; The Art Institute of Chicago (Photograph © 1993 all rights resvered) for pp. 20 and 42 (Collection Mr. and Mrs. Potter Palmer); The Burrell Collection (© Glasgow Museums) for pp. 27 and 88; Courtesy of The Fogg Art Museum, Harvard University Art Museums (Gift of the Friends of the Fogg Art Museum) for p. 68; Foundation E.G. Bührle Collection, Zurich for p. 45; Le Musée du Petit Palais, Paris for p. 32 (Photographie Giraudon) and p. 35 (Musées de la Ville de Paris © by S.P.A.D.E.M.); The Metropolitan Museum of Art, New York for p. 26; The Minneapolis Institute of Arts for p. 41 (given by Anne Pierce Rogers in memory of John DeCoster Rogers); Musée des Beaux-Arts, Nancy (G. Mangin) for p. 65; Musée de Picardie, Amiens (Claude Gheerbrant) for p. 58; Musée Toulouse-Lautrec, Albi for p. 50; The National Gallery of Art, Washington D.C. for p. 24; National Gallery of Scotland (Antonia Reeve) for p. 74; National Museum, Stockholm for p. 19; Philadelphia Museum of Art for p. 85; © The Phillips Collection, Washington D.C. for p. 16; Royal Academy of Arts, London for p. 72; The Shelburne Museum, Vermont for p. 30; Städtische Galerie, Städelsches Kunstinstitut (Artothek) for p. 38; Tate Gallery, London for pp. 62 and 77; The Wallraf-Richartz Museum, Cologne (Rheinischen Bildarchiv) for p. 31; Walters Art Gallery, Baltimore for p. 22; Yale University Art Gallery (The Katherine Ordway Collection) for p. 80; pp. 12 and 15 are reproduced by courtesy of the Trustees, The National Gallery, London; p. 55 is from *The Art of Cuisine* (Alex Saunderson) Courtesy of the Bibiotheque National, Paris; pp. 46 and 57 are courtesy of Terra Museum of American Art, Chicago (Daniel J. Terra Collection — © all rights reserved. Jerry Kobylecky, photographer); p. 71 is courtesy of the Museum of Fine Arts, Boston. The Index was prepared by Atlantic Union.

Bibliography

Beck, Simone; Bertholle, Louisette; Child, Julia. *Mastering the Art of French Cooking*. London, 1963.

David, Elizabeth. *French Provincial Cooking*. London, 1961.

Fisher, M. F. K. *The Art of Eating,* New York, 1976.

Grigson, Jane. *Charcuterie and French Pork Cookery*. London, 1967.

Joyant, Maurice; Toulouse-Lautrec, Henri de. *The Art of Cuisine,* London, 1966.

Hackforth-Jones, Jocelyn. *À Table avec les Impressionistes*. Paris, 1991.

Herbert, Robert L. *Impressionism, Art, Leisure and Parisian Society*. London, 1988.

Higgonet, Anne. *Berthe Morisot*. London, 1990.

Higgonet, Anne. *Berthe Morisot's Images of Women*. Cambridge Mass. London, 1992.

Holt, Geraldene. *French Country Kitchen*. London, 1987.

Joyes, Claire. *Les Carnets de Cuisine de Monet*. Paris, 1989.

La Mazille. *La Bonne Cuisine du Périgord*. Paris, 1929.

MacDonald, Margaret. *Whistler's Mother's Cook Book*. London, 1979.

Olney, Richard. *Simple French Food*. London, 1984.

Pomiane, Édouard de. *Radio Cuisine*. Paris, 1933.

Reboul, J. B. *La Cuisinière Provençale*. Marseille.

Rouart, Denis. *Correspondance de Berthe Morisot avec sa Famille et ses Amis*. Paris, 1950.

"Tante Marie." *La Véritable Cuisine de Famille*.

Toklas, Alice B. *The Alice B. Toklas Cook Book*. London, 1961.

Willan, Anne. *French Regional Cooking*. London, 1981.

Wolfert, Paula. *The Cooking of South West France*. London, 1987.

Index

mint 64, 81
Monet, Camille 39, 43, 67
Monet, Claude 7, 8, 9, 11, 12, 39, 43, 63, 67, 68, 70, 75; *10, 12, 38, 41, 45, 66, 68, 70, 72*
Monet, Jean 39, 43; *63*
Montparnasse 9
Moore, George 25, 33; *27*
Morisot, Berthe 8, 9, 25, 33, 34, 43, 47, 68; *32, 46*
Morisot, Edma 33
Morisot, Julie 34, 68; *32*
mushrooms 18; dried 18
mussels 36
mustard powder 88

nutmeg 13, 21, 52, 55, 65, 89
Nabis, the 63, 79, 91
Natanson, Thadée and Misia 8, 79; *50*
Normandy 39, 40

oil 91: olive oil 34, 35, 36, 53, 60, 69, 91; hazelnut 64; grape seed oil 84, 91
olives, black 60, 69; pitted green 52, 53
onions 13, 34, 35, 44, 53, 81; pickling 18; red 60
orange zest 54
Orpen, William 8; *72*

pancakes 84
pancetta 76, 90; see also bacon
paprika 65
Paris 7, 11, 17, 23, 33, 43, 47, 79; *27*
parsley 36, 37, 53, 60, 69, 76, 81, 88
parsnips 37
pâté 13, 64; *77*
peas 81
peppers: green, red, yellow 60
peppercorns (black) 13, 48
pheasant 39, 40; *41*

pigeons 52
Pissaro, Camille 8, 75; *74, 77*
Pissaro, Manzana 9
polenta 19, 92
pork: belly 13; fatty 76; ground fat 52; shoulder 13; tenderloin 26
Post-Impressionist 14
pot-au-feu 43
potatoes 30, 37, 52, 60; mashed 53; new 81
praline 25, 26
prosciutto crudo 44
prunes 25, 26

quinces 40

rabbit (wild) 31
radishes 60
Renoir, Pierre-Auguste 8, 12, 17; *16, 19, 20*
rice 19, 53
risotto rice 34
Ritz, Cesar 25
rosemary 52, 73, 81
rosewater 70
Roussel, Ker-Xavier 79
rum 61

sage 52
salad 14, 60, 64, 91; *84*
salmon 30; *30*
sandwiches 12, 87, 88
sauce: sorrel 30; tomato 65
semolina 48, 49
sformata 20, 92
shallots 52, 88
Sisley, Alfred 8, 43; *19, 45*
sorrel 30
soufflé 20, 21, 92
soup 30, 43, 48; chilled 48; Potage Bonne Femme 34, 37, 90
squabs 52

Stein, Gertrude 12, 87
stock 30, 34, 35, 37; chicken 18; home-made 52
strawberries 64
sugar 25, 54, 56, 61, 65, 70, 92; icing 35; vanilla 61, 64, 65, 84

"Tante Marie" 8, 79
tarragon 14, 48, 55
tarte 64
thyme 13, 18, 44, 48, 53, 76
Toklas, Alice B. 8, 12, 87, 88
tomatoes 34, 35, 36, 48, 49, 53, 60, 65, 69; sun-dried 88
Toulouse-Lautrec, Henri de 8, 34, 51, 52, 70; *50, 55, 72*
tuiles (cookies) 35, 54
tuna 60

vanilla 56
veal, ground 52
vegetables 75, 87, 90; puréed/sieved 37
venison, stewing 44
Villeneuve-sur-Yonne *14, 50*
vinegar: balsamic 64, 90; wine 60
Vuillard, Édouard 8, 79, 80, 91; *14, 50, 78, 80, 82-83, 84*

Walter, Martha *57*
whisky 40
Whistler, James Abbott McNeill 8, 70; *72*
wine: Beaumes de Venise 54; burgundy 44; Montbazillac 54; red 13, 18, 73; Vouvray 26; white 13, 14, 36, 53, 54, 76, 81

yoghurt 52

Zola, Emile 7
Zucchini, see courgette

The numbers in *italic* refer to illustration captions.